FIELD TRIPS

The Airport

Stuart A. Kallen
ABDO & Daughters

Published by Abdo & Daughters, 4940 Viking Drive, Suite 622, Edina, Minnesota 55435.

Copyright © 1997 by Abdo Consulting Group, Inc., Pentagon Tower, P.O. Box 36036, Minneapolis, Minnesota 55435 USA. International copyrights reserved in all countries. No part of this book may be reproduced in any form without written permission from the publisher.

Printed in the United States.

Cover and Interior Photo credits: Archive Photos
Wide World Photos
Illustration: Ben Dann Lander
Edited by Julie Berg

Library of Congress Cataloging-in-Publication Data

Kallen, Stuart A., 1955-
　　The airport / Stuart A. Kallen.
　　　　p.　cm. — (Field trips)
Includes index.
Summary: Describes the organization of the airport and the work which is performed there.
ISBN 1-56239-711-7
1. Airports—Juvenile literature. [1. Airports.] I. Title. II. Series.
TL725.15.K35 1997
387.7'36—dc20　　　　　　　　　　　　　96-18871
　　　　　　　　　　　　　　　　　　　　CIP
　　　　　　　　　　　　　　　　　　　　AC

Contents

Cities for People Who Fly

Is that a giant bird up in the sky? No. It's a jet airplane. And it's half as big as a football field. Where can a plane that big take off and land? At an airport, of course.

When you visit an airport, you'll see amazing things. You'll see giant planes that can hold 400 people. You'll be one of the 75,000 **passengers** that pass through an airport in a single day. Airplanes from all over the world take off and land every few minutes. You'll see people from far away places like Africa, Europe, and Asia. Thousands of tons of **cargo** will be loaded and unloaded while you are there.

You'll walk through the **terminal** where people wait for their flights. You'll see the areas where **baggage** is handled. And you'll see the big buildings on the edge of the **runways** called **hangars**. That's where airplanes are fixed and stored.

An airport is like a small city. It has its own police force, jail, fire station, and hospital. You will also see the airport shops, offices, buses, and taxis. Some airports are bigger than cities. Denver's International Airport is twice the size of New York City!

A cargo plane being loaded during the night.

Catching a Plane

Airports are not just for airplanes, they're for people too. When you arrive at an airport, you'll see many large buildings. Some are for people who are flying within the country. Some are for people flying to foreign countries.

The **terminal** buildings have rows of check-in desks for each airline. **Passengers** hand their tickets to airline workers using computers. Then their **baggage** is checked. The bags are weighed, given a number, and sent to the right airplane.

All passengers get boarding passes that allow them on their flights. Then they must enter the **concourse** and go to the gates from which their airplanes depart. To do this, all passengers must go through **security**.

Airports and planes are meant to be safe places for passengers. Security is tight. All passengers must go through a **metal detector** and have their bags X-rayed. Security officers look for weapons which are never

allowed on airplanes. Don't make any jokes while waiting
to go through the **metal detectors**. Keeping planes safe
is no joke.

People waiting in line at a busy airport.

Take Off!

The best part about a visit to the airport is watching the planes take off. As soon as every **passenger** is aboard the plane, the door is shut tight. Then the captain and crew begin a series of equipment checks.

The captain asks the **control tower** for permission to start engines. If the ground crew is out of the way, permission is granted. The captain asks to move to the **taxiway**. Finally the pilot moves the plane to the end of the **runway**. Air Traffic Control gives permission for take off.

The captain makes final checks and opens up the engines. The airplane races down the runway and takes off into the sky. A large jet needs two miles (3.2 km) of runway to take off.

Once in the sky, the captain cuts back on the engines to reduce noise until the plane is clear of the city.

Opposite page: A jet liner taking off.

Control Tower

Airplanes must take off and land into the wind. In most places the wind often comes from one or two directions. Airports build several **runways** that face the main winds. This makes it easier for the airplane to take off. The runways are linked by **taxiways** where airplanes wait to take off.

Pilots who fly airplanes cannot take off and land alone. They need help from people and computers in the **control tower**. There, air traffic controllers watch the movement of all aircraft on the runways and taxiways. Controllers use computers to plan the exact route of each plane as it moves through the airport. Controllers talk with the pilot by radio. They also direct crews on the ground. This is a very difficult task when many airplanes are taking off and landing at once.

In an emergency, controllers call up fire fighters, ambulances, rescue workers, and other people to help.

Air traffic controllers watch the planes from the control tower.

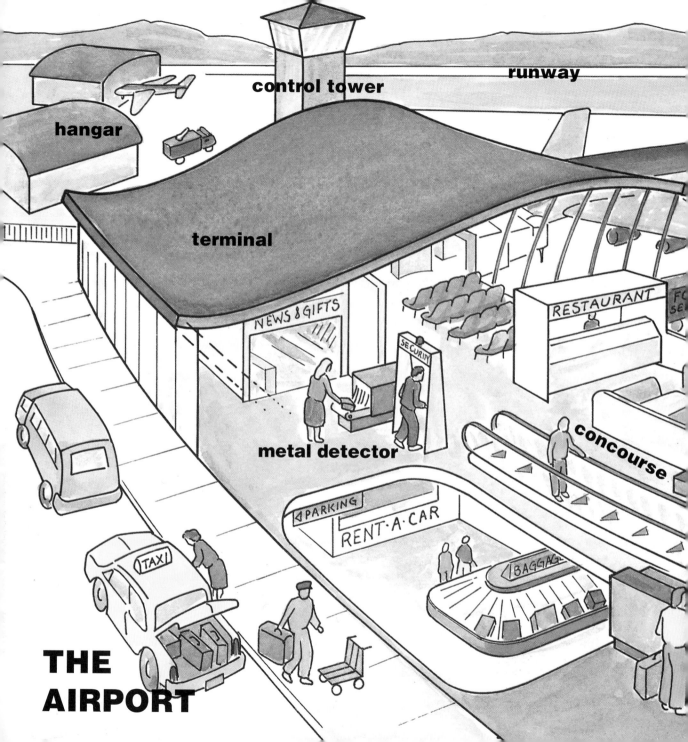

control tower

runway

hangar

terminal

NEWS & GIFTS

SECURITY

RESTAURANT

FOOD SERV

metal detector

concourse

PARKING

RENT·A·CAR

BAGGAGE

TAXI

THE AIRPORT

runway

taxi way

ground crew

FUEL

GATE 6B

gate

TICKETS

WORLD AIR

ARRIVALS

DEPARTURES

check-in desks

Landing

As the plane nears the end of its flight, the pilot contacts the **control tower**. There are usually many planes waiting to land. As the plane approaches the airport, a computer on the ground guides it toward the **runway**. A controller operates the computer to make sure it is working correctly.

Control towers use an **instrument landing system** (ILS) to land airplanes. Radio signals from the ground move two needles on the pilot's instruments. When the needles form a cross, the plane is lined up correctly. Red and white runway lights signal if the plane is too high or low.

Two pilots in the cockpit of a jetliner.

Once the plane has landed, it must go to an arrival gate. There, ground crews go to work while **passengers** leave the plane and enter the **concourse** to get their luggage.

When a jet liner lands, the pilot puts on the brakes to slow down the huge airplane.

15

Servicing the Airplane

Ground crews prepare the plane for its next flight. **Baggage** handlers with special trucks unload bags and other **cargo**. Cleaning staff will board the plane to clean up. Food handlers will stock the plane with meals and drinks to be served on the next flight.

After each flight, the captain writes a flight report. Mechanics check many parts of the plane. They check the engines, the electric systems, the lights, tires, and brakes. The engineer in charge will not allow the plane to leave the ground unless everything is working right.

Another mechanic checks the airplane's fuel. They make sure the fuel is clean because dirt could clog up the fuel pipes. The plane is refueled from a large tanker truck. A large jet plane holds up to 25,000 gallons (95,000 liters) of fuel.

Jets are washed often to prevent drag on the plane.

The City That Never Sleeps

After the airplane is serviced, a new pilot and crew climb aboard. And the giant jet is ready to fly again.

What you see in one day at the airport is repeated 365 days a year. The airport is a giant city all by itself—a giant city that never sleeps.

Opposite page: A flight attendant (center) with two pilots after a flight.

Glossary

baggage - Suitcases and luggage people carry their belongings in when they travel.

cargo - loads of mail, packages, and goods carried by an airplane.

co-pilot - the man or woman who helps a captain fly an airplane.

concourse - the long hallway with many airplane gates.

control tower - the glass tower at an airport where air traffic controllers guide airplanes on their flights.

flight attendant - women or men who help passengers on the airplane.

hangars - large garages where airplanes are parked and serviced.

instrument landing system (ILS) - the computerized landing system that guides airplanes into airports using radio beacons.

metal detector - an instrument that can tell if a person is carrying a knife or a gun.

passenger - a person who rides on an airplane.

runway - long paved roads that airplanes take off and land on.

security - something or someone that makes a place safe from harm.

taxiways - roads that connect runways at an airport.

terminal - a large building that handles transportation lines.

Index

J

jail 5

L

landing 10
lights 16
luggage 15

M

mechanics 16
metal detector 6

N

New York City 5

O

offices 5

P

passengers 4, 6, 15
pilot 8, 14
police 5

R

radio 10
radio signals 14
rescue workers 10

runway

runway 5, 8, 10, 14
runway lights 14

S

security 6
shops 5

T

takeoff 8, 10
tanker truck 16
taxis 5
taxiway 8, 10
terminal 4, 6
tickets 6
tires 16

W

wind 10